English

Ages 7-9

Key Stage 2

PaRragon

Bath · New York · Singapore · Hong Kong · Cologne · Delhi
Melbourne · Amsterdam · Johannesburg · Auckland · Shenzhen

This edition published by Parragon in 2012
Parragon
Queen Street House
4 Queen Street
Bath BA1 1HE, UK
www.parragon.com

Copyright © Parragon Books Ltd 2009

Written by; Nina Filipek
Consultant checked by; Martin Malcolm
Illustrated by; Rob Davis/www.the-art-agency.co.uk
and Tom Connell/www.the-art-agency.co.uk

ISBN 978-1-4454-7756-5

Printed in China

Parents' page

The Gold Stars® Key Stage 2 series has been created to help your child revise and practise key skills and information learned in school. Each book is a complete companion to the Key Stage 2 curriculum and has been written by an expert team of teachers. The books will help to prepare your child for the SATs in year 6 and other tests that children take in school.

The books also support Scottish National Guidelines 5-14.

How to use this book

- Talk through the introductions to each topic and review the examples together.

- Encourage your child to tackle the fill-in activities independently.

- Keep work times short. Skip a page if it seems too difficult and return to it later.

- It doesn't matter if your child does some of the pages out of order.

- Answers to questions don't need to be complete sentences.

- Check the answers on pages 60-63. Encourage effort and reward achievement with praise.

- If your child finds any of the pages too difficult, don't worry. Children learn at different rates.

Contents

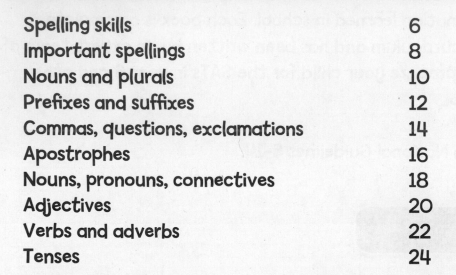

Spelling, grammar and punctuation

Reading comprehension

Fiction

Non-fiction

Writing composition

Fiction

Non-fiction

Spelling skills

One way of learning to spell a new word is by using these 5 steps.

1. Look at the word
2. Say it
3. Cover it
4. Write it
5. Check it

Look for common letter patterns to spell these groups of words.

could, should, would	found, ground, loud, shout
clown, frown, town	coin, noise, soil, voice
bridge, fudge, hedge	cuddle, middle, little, table

A Sometimes you can find a root word or a word within a word.

Underline the root word in each of these groups of words.

<u>cook</u>	<u>cook</u>er	<u>cook</u>ery ✓
<u>spark</u>	<u>spark</u>le	<u>spark</u>ler ✓
<u>clear</u>	<u>clear</u>ed	<u>clear</u>ly ✓
<u>bed</u>room	<u>bed</u>stead	<u>bed</u>time ✓
<u>sign</u>	<u>sign</u>al	<u>sign</u>ature ✓

Do I have a tale or a tail?

you have a tail

B

Homophones are tricky words that sound the same but are spelled differently.

Write the correct homophone in each space below.

hear or here	ate or eight
right or write	beech or beach
would or wood	where, were or wear

1. Teri is nearly __eight__ years old. ✓
2. I couldn't __hear__ what she said. ✓
3. I don't know if it's the __right__ way. ✓
4. __would__ you like to sleep over at my house? ✓
5. __Where__ can I get the bus into town? ✓
6. We made sandcastles on the __beach__. ✓

List any other homophones that you know:

This is an example of a mnemonic; this **hear** has an **ear** in it!

Important spellings

Learning objective: to learn to spell frequently used words

Learn to spell words that you often need to read and write. For example, days of the week, months of the year and words for numbers.

A

Write the names of the days of the week:

Today is _____Sunday_____ ✓.
Yesterday was _____Saturday_____ ✓.
Tomorrow is _____Monday_____ ✓.

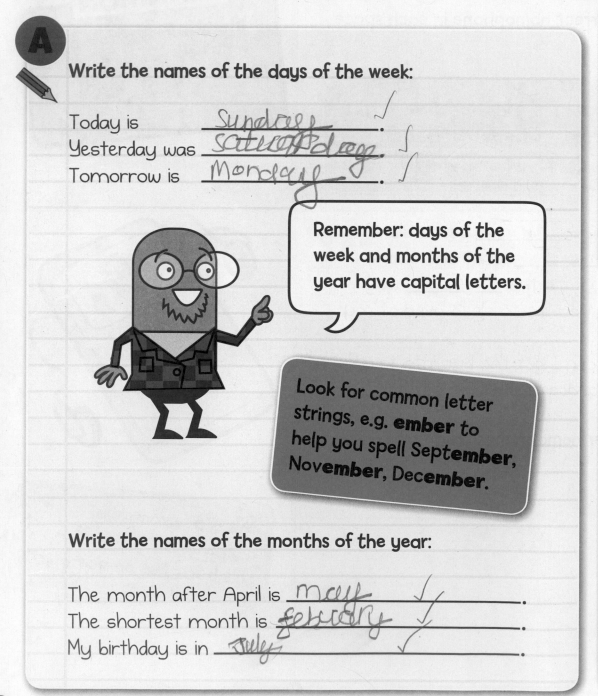

Remember: days of the week and months of the year have capital letters.

Look for common letter strings, e.g. **ember** to help you spell Sept**ember**, Nov**ember**, Dec**ember**.

Write the names of the months of the year:

The month after April is _____May_____ ✓.
The shortest month is _____february_____ ✓.
My birthday is in _____July_____ ✓.

Days of the week

Monday
Tuesday
Wednesday
Thursday
Friday
Saturday
Sunday

Months of the year

January
February
March
April
May
June
July
August
September
October
November
December

Don't forget that place names always start with capital letters.

Use **look**, **say**, **cover**, **write**, **check** to learn these ordinal numbers.

first, second, third, fourth, fifth, sixth, seventh, eighth, ninth, tenth

B

Write the ordinal numbers, e.g. first, second.

1st _first_ ✓
2nd _second_ ✓
3rd _third_ ✓
4th _fourth_ ✓
5th _fifth_ ✓
6th _sixth_ ✓
7th _seventh_ ✓
8th _eighth_ ✓
9th _ninth_ ✓
10th _tenth_ ✓

Learn to spell words that often appear in addresses. For example:

| Street | Avenue | Close |
| Road | Lane | Drive |

C

Write your home address:
273 Dyce Way
_Ky> 6uX_ ✓

Now write your school address:
Magnus drive
_Ky> 6Tr_ ✓

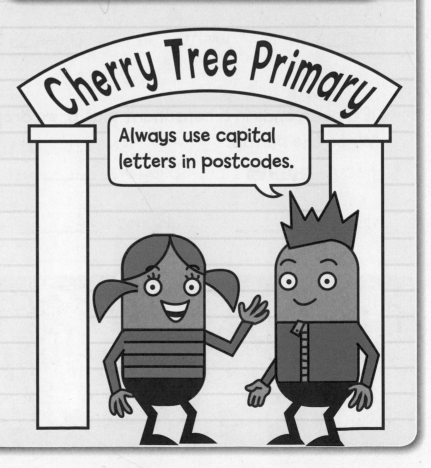

Cherry Tree Primary

Always use capital letters in postcodes.

Nouns and Plurals

Learning objective: to learn plural forms of words

A **noun** is a person, a place or a thing. Nouns can be **singular** (only one) or **plural** (more than one).

A

When we make most words plural we add an **s** to the end. Write the plurals.

sausage**s** ✓   cake**s** ✓   drink**s** ✓

book**s** ✓   horse**s** ✓   tree**s** ✓

But if a word ends in **ch, sh, s, ss** or **x** we usually add **es**. Write the plurals.

dish**es** ✓   kiss**es** ✓   fox**es** ✓   lunch**es** ✓

bus**es** ✓   wish**es** ✓   cross**es** ✓

If a noun ends in a consonant plus **y**, we drop the **y** and write **ies**. Write the plurals.

pony > **ponies**   baby > **ies** ✓   story > **ies** ✓

daisy > **ies** ✓   cherry > **ies** ✓   berry > **ies** ✓

Some tricky plurals don't follow the rules. Learn them by heart.

man > men   child > children   leaf > leaves
mouse > mice   goose > geese   person > people

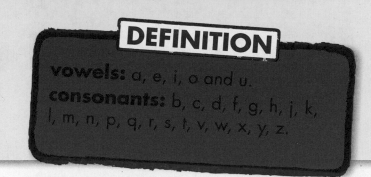

DEFINITION

vowels: a, e, i, o and u.
consonants: b, c, d, f, g, h, j, k, l, m, n, p, q, r, s, t, v, w, x, y, z.

B

Read the poem below and turn the singular nouns into plurals. Mostly you can just add **s** but sometimes you have to rewrite the word in the space.

I Love the Seasons

I love it in the spring when the **bud** _s_ burst into **million** _s_ of tiny **flower** _s_ . ∫

I love it in the summer when we can make **sandcastle** _s_ on the beach. /

I love it in the autumn when the **leaf** _leaves_ on the **tree** _s_ turn from / green to gold.

Best of all, I love it in the winter when we can make **snowman** _snowmen_ . ∫

The words **sheep, deer** and **fish** stay the same whether they are singular or plural.

C

Change the nouns in bold in these sentences to plurals.

1. There is a **mouse** in the house! › There are _mice_ in the house! ✓

2. There was only one **loaf**. › There were only two _loaves_ . ✓

3. We saw a **goose** in the park. › We saw _Geese_ in the park. ✓

11

Prefixes are extra letters added to the beginning of words. They change the meaning of the root word.

For example:

The rabbit appeared, then **dis**appeared, then **re**appeared!

A

Writing **un** at the beginning of these words will change their meaning. Try it and see!

untie   **un**fair ✓
unlock ✓   **un**do ✓
unlike ✓   **un**lucky ✓
unlikely ✓   **un**happy ✓
unable ✓   **un**hurt ✓

Choose three words from the lists above to complete the dialogue below. Write the words in the spaces.

Tom's mum: I'm very _unhappy_ with you. ✓

Tom: It's so _unfair_ ! It wasn't my fault. ✓

I'm just _unlucky_ ! ✓

DEFINITION

prefixes: the extra letters added to the beginning of a word.
suffixes: the extra letters added to the end of a word.

B

Underline words with prefixes in this passage. Look for **dis, re, im, un.**

Tom and Jez went to see a <u>re</u>make of *Monsters of the Deep.* Writing about it in a movie <u>re</u>view for their school magazine, they said, "The monsters were <u>un</u>realistic and <u>un</u>imaginative really. There was lots of action but the plot was <u>dis</u>jointed and <u>im</u>possible to follow."

Suffixes are extra letters added to the end of words. Look at how they change the meaning of the root word.

The word **unsuccessful** has a prefix *and* a suffix!

For example:

hope > hopeless > hopeful   care > careful > careless

use > useful > useless   thought > thoughtful > thoughtless

C

Choose a suffix to make sense of these sentences.
Write **less** or **ful**.

1. It was very thought<u>ful</u> of Jenny to buy flowers.
2. The toy was use<u>less</u> without a battery.
3. I felt hope<u>ful</u> at the start but then everything went wrong!
4. I knew I had to be care<u>ful</u> this time.

Commas, questions, exclamations

Commas tell readers to pause and take a moment to understand what a sentence is about.

- Put a comma after each item of a list.
- Never put a comma before the word 'and'.
- Put a comma after a group of words that belong together.

How to use commas:
- After each item in a list.
- To separate ideas within a sentence.

For example:

The huge plate was piled high with bacon, egg, mushrooms, fried onions, black pudding, baked beans and tomato!

A

Write the commas in these sentences.

1. We'll have two cornets, with raspberry sauce, a vanilla ice cream, a carton of orange juice and a cup of tea please.

2. I'd like to order the tomato soup, an egg and cress sandwich, a banana smoothie and a chocolate muffin please.

B

Write commas in these long sentences to separate the different ideas and make the text easier to read. The commas go where you pause when you read aloud.

1. The cat ran up the stairs, down the corridor, through the classroom and into Mrs Worgan's office!

2. Go right at the lights, turn right again at the T-junction, then first left.

> Sentences that ask questions usually begin with **What**, **When**, **Where**, **Why** or **How**.

Exclamation marks (!) show surprise and excitement.
Question marks (?) are used at the end of sentences when a question is asked.

C

Read the sentences below and decide whether to write an exclamation mark or a question mark in each one.

1. Suddenly, all the lights went out__!__
2. "Aaaaaaaargh__!__" he cried.
3. Gina called out, "Hey, Tom__!__"
4. "What are 'gators__?__" she asked.
5. How do we know there's no life on Mars__?__

Speech marks highlight words that are spoken.

For example:

"How many children are coming?" asked Jason.

How to use speech marks:
- Open the speech marks at the start and close them at the end of the words spoken.
- All other punctuation goes inside the speech marks.

D

Write the speech marks in the sentences below.

1. Tara cried, "Wait for me!"
2. "Do you think he's an elf?" said Taylor.
3. "Okay," said Sharon. "What's wrong?"
4. "Wow!" said Zac. "You're a genius!"

15

Apostrophes

Apostrophes can shorten words or tell you to whom something belongs.

An apostrophe can replace missing letters:

> For example:
>
> do not > don't   it is > it's
>
> we are > we're   they will > they'll

Apostrophes are tricky! Keep practising until you understand how they work.

A

Shorten these words by using apostrophes.

cannot > **can't**   could not > Couldn't

should not > Shouldn't   we will > We'll

they will > They'll   where is > Where's

she is > She's   they are > They're

Apostrophes can also show possession.

> For example: Ben's shoes.

B

Rewrite each of these phrases using an apostrophe.

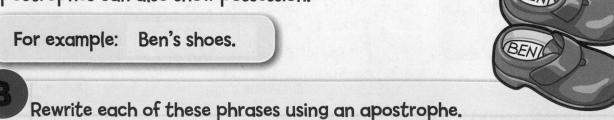

1. The shoes belonging to Ben **Ben's shoes**
2. The book belonging to my friend My friend's book
3. The lead belonging to the dog The dog's lead
4. The car belonging to Joe Joe's car
5. The whiskers belonging to the cat The cat's whiskers

16

The possessive apostrophe can also tell you how many there are.

For example:

1.	The boy's trainers were new. (one boy)
2.	The boys' trainers were new. (more than one boy)

Remember these exceptions – the children's clothes, the men's clothes, the people's clothes.

If the noun is singular the apostrophe goes before the s.
If the noun is plural the apostrophe goes after the s.

C

Rewrite each of these phrases using a possessive apostrophe.

1.	The fish belonging to the girl.

	The girl's fish

2.	The book belonging to the teacher.

3.	The television belonging to the family.

4.	The red nose belonging to the clown.

5.	The pram belonging to the babies.

6.	The house belonging to the dolls.

7.	The drawings belonging to the children.

8.	The race belonging to the men.

DEFINITION

To 'possess' means to 'own'.
Possessive apostrophes:
These are used to show who owns a particular thing.

Learning objective: to recognize nouns, pronouns, connectives

A **noun** is a naming word. It can be a person, place or thing.

For example:

| The bee buzzed. **bee** is a noun. | Richard ran away. **Richard** is a noun. | The cats miaowed loudly. **cats** is a noun. |

A Underline the nouns in these sentences:

The flowers were pretty.   I live in London.   The food was delicious.
Zak was asleep.   The girls laughed.   My sister has a laptop.

A **pronoun** is a word you can use to replace a noun so that you don't have to repeat it.

For example: Connor is kind. > He is kind.   **He** is a pronoun.

B Rewrite these sentences using pronouns.

Choose from this list: him   she   it   they   them   we

1. The flowers were pretty so I put the flowers in a vase.
   The flowers were pretty so I put <u>them</u> in a vase.

2. Zak was asleep so I didn't want to wake Zak up.

3. I like London because London has an interesting history.

4. The girls laughed because the girls thought it was funny.

5. Chris and I went swimming. Chris and I had a great time.

Noun: A person, a place or a thing.
Pronoun: A word you can use instead of the noun.
Connective: A word that links ideas, sentences and paragraphs together.

Connectives are words that link ideas, sentences and paragraphs. Here are some useful connectives:

first, next, finally, consequently, later, suddenly, except, meanwhile, however, when, but, before, and, after, although, also, then

C

Choose connectives from the list above to complete this school diary.

Taylor's school diary: Tuesday

First , after register we had a spelling test. _____ we wrote animal poems. _____ lunch, we had a visitor.
It was Mrs White. She'd brought her new baby to show us.
_____ lunch, we had games outside on the field.
_____ , _____ it started to rain and we had to run inside. _____ , it was our science lesson. _____ , just before home time we had a story.

D

Now write your diary for yesterday in the space below. Choose connectives to link your ideas and sentences together.

Yesterday I woke up at...

Adjectives

Learning objective: to learn to use adjectives

Adjectives are used to describe people, places or things.

For example:

a **large** dog

a **small** dog

A Sort these adjectives into three groups. Write them below each group heading.

blue	average	excitable
violet	sullen	bored
indigo	raucous	scarlet
huge	angry	ginormous
miniscule	lemon	narrow

Colours: Sizes: Moods:

blue

B

Write a similar adjective (a **synonym**) for these common adjectives.

1. We had a nice time.
   We had a <u>great</u> time.
2. The pizza was okay.

3. The giant stomped his big foot.

4. It was a funny movie.

This activity is the opposite of difficult. It's **easy!**

Opposite adjectives are known as **antonyms**.

C

Write an antonym for each of these adjectives.

black > **white**

bold > _____

hazy > _____

hairy > _____

unusual > _____

scorching > _____

expensive > _____

popular > _____

delicious > _____

polite > _____

D

Change these adjectives to alter the meaning of the sentences.

1. A friendly, little dog came bounding up to her.

   A _____, _____ dog came bounding up to her.

2. It was an antique table.

   It was a _____ table.

3. It was a difficult job.

   It was an _____ job.

4. He was in a happy mood.

   He was in a _____ mood.

5. She went red when she saw him.

   She went _____ when she saw him.

DEFINITION

synonym: A word with a similar meaning.
antonym: A word with an opposite meaning.

V r s --n -- v r s

Learning objective: to learn to use verbs and adverbs

A verb is an action word. A sentence should have a verb.

> For example: The alien **jumped** up behind them and **burped**!

A Underline the verbs in these sentences.

1. The mouse found the cheese.

2. The cat chased the mouse.

3. The frog leaped into the pond.

4. The boy ate the chocolate bar.

5. The car skidded round the bend and crashed.

> Which sentence has two verbs?

B Change the verbs in these sentences to alter the meaning.

1. The girl dropped the ice cream.
   The girl _____ the ice cream.

2. The red team won the race!
   The red team _____ the race!

3. The family loved camping.
   The family _____ camping.

4. The children baked a cake.
   The children _____ a cake.

5. The boy ran across the road.
   The boy _____ across the road.

DEFINITION

verb: A doing or action word.
sentence: A group of words that belong together.

You can **easily** do these exercises!

An **adverb** describes the verb.

For example:

The alien **suddenly** jumped up behind them and burped **loudly**!

C Underline the verbs in these sentences then circle the adverbs.

1. The cat purred softly.

2. The giant sneezed loudly.

3. The man drove quickly.

4. The sun beat fiercely.

5. She sang beautifully.

D Change the adverbs in these sentences to alter the meaning.

1. The teacher spoke sternly.
   The teacher spoke_____.

2. The boy carefully wrote his name.
   The boy _____ wrote his name.

3. The car quickly came to a halt.
   The car _____ came to a halt.

4. The children played noisily.
   The children played _____.

5. I sneezed uncontrollably.
   I sneezed _____.

DEFINITION

adverb: A word that describes a verb.

Tenses

The tense of the verbs in a sentence tells you when something happens.

It rained last night.

It's snowing now!

It will be cloudy tomorrow.

The weather forecast

Sat: sun	Tue: cloud
Sun: rain	Wed: rain
Mon: snow	Thurs: rain
	Fri: sun

A

Look at the weather forecast. Then write a sentence to answer each question.

1. What will the weather be like on Wednesday?

2. What was the weather like on Saturday?

3. What is the weather like today?

B

Write the past, present or future tense sentences to complete the chart.

Past	Present	Future
It was hot.	It is hot.	_____
I was hot.	_____	_____
_____	He is hot.	He will be hot.
_____	We are hot.	_____
_____	_____	They will be hot.

24

To find out more about suffixes turn to page 12.

A suffix can change the time from the present to the past:

Present	Present continuous	Past
I play.	I am playing.	I played.
I work.	I am working.	I worked.

C

Complete these present and past tense verbs.

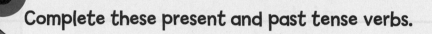

Present	Present continuous	Past
I paint.	I am paint____.	I paint____.
I jump.	I am jump____.	I jump____.
I shop.	I am shop____.	I shop____.
I skip.	I am skip____.	I skip____.

Irregular verbs don't follow the usual rules.
Learn them by heart.

Present	Past
I get	I got
I have	I had
I go	I went

D

Change the verbs in this story from the present tense to the past tense.

I get out of the car and step in a puddle. We hear the band playing. They have started already! I run all the way to the hall.

I ____ out of the car and _____ in a puddle. We ____ the band playing. They ____ started already! I ____ all the way to the hall.

Fiction and non-fiction

Fiction books contain made-up stories. Non-fiction books contain information and fact. Fiction and non-fiction books are written in different ways.

Fiction books usually have:
- dialogue
- characters
- a story or plot
- illustrations

Non-fiction books usually have:
- information and facts
- photographs
- diagrams or maps
- an index

A

Label these book titles as either F for fiction or NF for non-fiction. Write in the box next to each one.

How Volcanoes Work ☐   Teddy Goes to Toytown ☐

Primary Science ☐   A History of the Vikings ☐

Bedtime Stories ☐   Treasure Island ☐

DEFINITION

dialogue: Conversation and words that are spoken.

index: An alphabetical list of things in a book, with the page numbers on which each one appears, to make it easy to find things. Look at the index on page 64 of this book.

My book is called *Morris and the Aliens*. Do you think it is fiction or non-fiction?

Sort your books at home into fiction and non-fiction collections.

B

Read the texts A, B and C extracted from different books and match them to the correct book titles below:

Disappearing Worlds   Wizardy Woo   Secrets and Spies

A. It was on the night of the next full moon that things began to go wrong. Spells that had worked perfectly well for hundreds of years had suddenly lost their magic....

From title: _____

B. Supergirl sped past the secret agents in her souped-up spy car. She had to reach Point Blank before they did. Her secret life depended on it!

From title: _____

C. The world's rainforests are vitally important to us. But every hour, thousands of square kilometres of trees are being cut down all over the world.

From title: _____

C

Which of these books would be in the fiction section and which in the non-fiction section of a library? Write the titles in the correct columns.

Fiction   Non-fiction

Read the passage below and answer the questions about it.

Sale starts today

Anxious faces peer in through the shop window.

Inside, the manager's forehead wrinkles as she frowns. The 'SALE!' sign on the rack keeps falling off. Her fingers fumble as she hurriedly tapes the sign back in place.

As the crowd gathers outside, like sharks around a carcass, the shop assistants stare anxiously out. They dread the store opening.

The manager smoothes out the creases in her skirt and buttons her jacket. She takes a deep breath and walks towards the doors. With each step she feels like an underwater swimmer moving against the current.

Click! The key opens the lock and the doors bang open. The manager is pushed back, like a seashell carried on a wave, as people surge through the shop doors. The mayhem begins.

Remember: a simile is when we say that something is like something else.

A Write a sentence to answer each question.

1. What do you think the story is about?

2. Who is waiting outside the shop?

3. How do you think the manager is feeling?

4. What simile is used to describe the masses gathered outside?

5. Which two similes are used to describe the manager?

6. What mayhem is about to begin?

7. Write an alternative title for the story.

Fables

A fable is a short story with a moral lesson. The characters in fables are often animals.

A In Aesop's fable of 'The Dog and His Bone' below, some words have been left out. Predict what the words might be and write them in the spaces.

A dog was hurrying home with a big bone _____ the butcher had given him. He growled at everyone _____ passed, worried that they might try to steal it _____ him. He planned to bury the bone in the _____ and eat it later.

As he crossed a bridge _____ a stream, the dog happened to look down into _____ water. There he saw another dog with a much _____ bone. He didn't realize he was looking at his _____ reflection! He growled at the other dog and it _____ back.

The greedy dog wanted that bone, too, and _____ snapped at the dog in the water. But then _____ own big bone fell into the stream with a _____ , and quickly sank out of sight. Then he realized _____ foolish he had been.

Who was Aesop?

Aesop was probably a Greek storyteller who lived over two thousand years ago.

Research some other Aesop's fables at your local library.

B

Write sentences to answer these questions about 'The Dog and His Bone'.

1. Why was the dog hurrying home?

2. Why did the other dog growl back?

3. What lesson do you think the dog learned?

4. What is the moral of the fable? Tick the correct answer, a, b or c.
   a) Waste not want not.
   b) It is foolish to be greedy.
   c) Be happy with how you look.

5. If you rewrote the fable using the same moral but a different animal character, which animal would you choose? Say why.

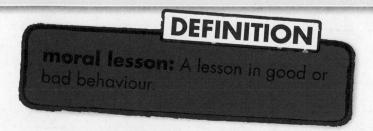

DEFINITION

moral lesson: A lesson in good or bad behaviour.

31

Alliteration

Learning objective: to recognize alliteration

Alliteration is when we put words together that start with the same sound.

For example: This monster movie is a massive hit.

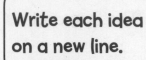
Write each idea on a new line.

A

Write a list poem, using alliteration.

One wiggly worm.

Two _____ _____

Three _____ _____

Four _____ _____

Five _____ _____

Six _____ _____

Seven _____ _____

Eight _____ _____

Nine _____ _____

Ten _____ _____

I'm jumping for joy! Is that an alliteration?

B

Complete the magazine headlines below using alliteration. Choose words from this list.

DOGS   LONG   TWOSOME   LOCKS   TERRIBLE   RECYCLE   DRAMA

REUSE AND _____

DANCING _____ **IN SCHOOL** _____

TWINS ARE A _____ _____

LOOK AFTER YOUR _____ _____

C

Complete these sentences using fun alliterations.

My alligator	is called Albert	and he's adorable.
My bear	is called Baloo	and he's big.
My c_____	is called C_____	and he's c_____ .
My d_____	is called D_____	and she's d_____ .
My e_____	is called E_____	and she's e_____ .
My f_____	is called F_____	and she's f_____ .

DEFINITION

alliteration: Words that begin with the same sounds.

Classic poetry

Learning objective: to understand different types of poems

Read this extract from 'The Pied Piper of Hamelin' by Robert Browning

Rats!
They fought the dogs, and killed the cats,
And bit the babies in the cradles,
And ate the cheeses out of the vats,
And licked the soup from the cook's own ladles,
Split open the kegs of salted sprats,
Made nests inside men's Sunday hats,
And even spoiled the women's chats,
By drowning their speaking
With shrieking and squeaking
In fifty different sharps and flats.

DEFINITION

classic: A classic is a great book or piece of writing usually from long ago.

A

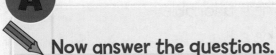

Now answer the questions.

1. What is the extract about?

2. Look at the first three lines. Which words are alliterations - that is, begin with the same sounds?

3. Find five words in the poem that rhyme with **cats**.

Robert Browning was a famous writer who lived 1812—1889.

4. What is a **ladle**?

5. How many cooks are there? What does the apostrophe in **cook's** tell us?

6. Why do you think the poet chose these three words: **speaking**, **shrieking** and **squeaking**?

7. What are **Sunday hats**?

8. Which two lines of the poem show that the rats make a tuneless and annoying noise?

9. If you've heard the story of the Pied Piper of Hamelin, write down what you know about it. If you're not familiar with the story, try to find a library copy.

DEFINITION

cradle: A small cot that swings.
sprat: A small fish.

Learning objective: to understand different types of poems

Read this nonsense poem and answer the questions below.

The Vulture
The Vulture eats between his meals
And that's the reason why
He very, very rarely feels
As well as you and I.

His eye is dull, his head is bald,
His neck is growing thinner.
Oh! what a lesson for us all
To only eat at dinner!

Hilaire Belloc

A

1. Which two words in the poem are on the ends of their lines, but do not actually rhyme?'

2. Why did the poet choose the word **thinner**?

3. What lesson does the poem teach us?

4. Do you think this is a serious poem? Explain your answer.

Read the limerick out loud. Which lines rhyme with which?

Read the limerick below and answer the questions.

There was a young lady of Twickenham
Whose boots were too tight to walk quickenham.
She bore them awhile,
But at last, at a stile,
She pulled them both off and was sickenham.

Anon

DEFINITION

nonsense poem: A poem that doesn't make sense.
limerick: A five-line comic poem with a rhyme pattern.
anon: Anonymous. It means that we don't know who wrote the poem because it was written a long time ago.

B

1. Why has the poet made up the words **quickenham** and **sickenham**?

2. What does **she bore them awhile** mean?

3. Write down a limerick that you know or make up one of your own.

Playscripts

Learning objective: to understand how to read a playscript

Read the playscript below.

Scene 1: A New Puppy
Two dogs talking in the park.
Characters:
   Buster: Bulldog
   Sindy: Yorkshire Terrier

BUSTER: (wailing) A new puppy! After everything I've done for them.

SINDY: I knew you'd be upset. I said to our Mindy when I heard.

BUSTER: I take them for lovely walks, I eat up all their leftovers – even that takeaway muck they always dish out on a Friday… and this is the thanks I get!

SINDY: (sympathetically) You can choose your friends but you can't choose your owners.

BUSTER: What can they want a puppy for anyway?

SINDY: Well, puppies are cute.

BUSTER: Cute! Aren't I cute enough for them?

SINDY: Er…

BUSTER: Well, I'm telling you now. It's not getting its paws on my toys. I've buried them all!

How to write a **playscript**:
• Write the speaker's name then what they say.
• Start a new line for each speaker.

How to write a **prose story**:
• Start a new paragraph for each speaker.
• Put speech marks around the words spoken and include the speaker's name in the sentence.

playscript: The text of a play, including a list of characters, what the actors say and their actions on stage.

A

Now rewrite the playscript as a prose story. Fill in the missing words.

Chapter 1: A New Puppy

"_____!" Buster wailed. "_____
_____."

"I knew you'd be upset," replied Sindy. "_____."

"I take them for lovely walks, I eat up all their leftovers – even that takeaway muck they always dish out on a Friday _____
_____!" said Buster.

"You can choose your friends but you can't choose your owners," _____.

"_____?" cried Buster.

"Well, puppies are cute," said Sindy.

"_____?" replied Buster.

"Er…" said Sindy.

"Well, I'm telling you now," said Buster. "_____
_____

Formal letters

Learning objective: to read and understand a formal letter

Read these formal letters and write a sentence to answer each question.

> 6 Acorn Avenue,
> Newbridge,
> N16 5BH
>
> Monday, 7 May 2012
>
> Dear Miss Grinstead,
>
> I would be grateful if you would allow Becky to leave school early tomorrow afternoon. She has an appointment at the dentist at 3.15 pm but I would need to pick her up from school at 2.45 pm. I'm sorry that she will miss the last lesson of the day but this was the only time available.
>
> As Tuesday is homework night, perhaps I could take Becky's homework with me when I come to collect her.
>
> Yours sincerely,
>
> Mrs Alice Kenwood

A

1. If Becky's appointment is at 3.15 pm why does she need to leave at 2.45 pm?

2. On what day of the week is Becky's appointment?

3. Why does Mrs Kenwood apologise for taking Becky early?

4. Becky thinks she won't have to do her homework. Is this true?

DEFINITION

formal letter: A business letter to someone who is not a personal friend.

Mrs A Kenwood,
6 Acorn Avenue,
Newbridge,
N16 5BH

Monday, 7 May 2012

Botchit Kitchens,
Dead End Lane,
Newbridge,
NO1 1N

Dear Sir,

I am writing to complain about your company's shoddy workmanship on my recently fitted new kitchen.

Firstly, all of the doors are hanging off their hinges. Secondly, the drawers have been fitted upside-down so we can't put anything in them. Thirdly, you forgot to make room for the sink! What use is a kitchen without a sink?

I want to know when you are able to put these things right. Please call me to arrange a time as soon as possible.

Yours faithfully,

B

1. Whose address is printed on the left-hand side of the page?

2. What does 'shoddy' mean in the first sentence?

3. What is the purpose of the letter?

4. From reading the letter, how do you think Mrs Kenwood is feeling?

Instructions

Learning objective: to understand instruction text

Read the instructions and then answer the questions below.

Apple and Raspberry Refresher

Ingredients (serves 1):
4 ice cubes
1 tablespoon raspberry syrup
250 ml or 8 fl oz apple juice
thin slices of apple for decoration

What you do:
1. Put the ice cubes in a plastic bag and crush them with a rolling pin.
2. Tip the ice into a glass.
3. Pour on the raspberry syrup.
4. Fill the glass to the top with apple juice.
5. Decorate with thin slices of apple.

A

1. What other things will you need in addition to the list of ingredients?

2. Is there enough for two glasses?

3. Do you need apple slices to make this drink?

4. The instructions include the following words: put, tip, pour, fill, decorate. Are these words nouns, verbs or adjectives?

5. Write an alternative name for this drink.

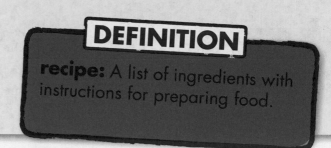

DEFINITION

recipe: A list of ingredients with instructions for preparing food.

Look at the recipe and read the instructions. Can you spot a missing ingredient?

Chicken Salad Supreme Sandwich

Ingredients:
bread
margarine
cooked chicken
lettuce leaves
tomatoes

What you do:
1. Butter the bread.
2. Put the chicken on the bread.
3. Spread on some mayonnaise.
4. Then add tomatoes and lettuce.
5. Then sandwich together.

This recipe is badly written because:
- The list of ingredients is incomplete.
- We don't know how much we need of anything.
- Some steps are missing from **What you do**.

B

Rewrite the recipe in your own words. Try to make big improvements on the original.

Read this page carefully, then write a sentence to answer each question about it on the opposite page.

The Spanish Armada

In 1587, Elizabeth I was Queen of England and Philip II was King of Spain. The two countries disagreed over religion. When Elizabeth signed a death warrant for the Catholic Mary Queen of Scots and was executed, it was the final straw for Philip. He ordered an invasion.

In 1588, Philip sent an Armada of 130 warships to invade England. But the English saw them coming and set sail, meeting the Spanish Armada in the English Channel. The Spanish ships sailed in a crescent shape around the English fleet. The English knew they would have to break this formation to defeat the Armada.

So the English sent burning ships to sail into the Spanish Armada. The plan worked and the Armada scattered. The Spanish ships were large, heavy and slow to move and turn. The English ships were smaller and could turn quickly. They had better cannons too, which caused a lot of damage to the Spanish ships.

The Armada tried to escape back to Spain by sailing north but bad weather blew the ships towards the coasts of Ireland and Scotland. Many ships were wrecked against the rocks.

Only half of the ships that set out in the Armada made it back to Spain. None of the English ships were lost. It was one of Elizabeth's greatest victories.

DEFINITION

crescent: A curved shape.
death warrant: An order to put somebody to death.
Catholic: A member of the Roman Catholic Church.

Information text is found in non-fiction books.

A

1. Why do you think Philip was angry when Mary Queen of Scots was executed?

2. What does 'this was the final straw for Philip' mean?

3. Why would a crescent shape of Spanish ships be a problem for the English?

4. How did the English plan to break up the Armada?

5. What advantages did the English ships have?

6. Where was the Armada shipwrecked?

7. Approximately how many Spanish ships survived the battle?

8. How many English ships survived?

Learning objective: to write a shape and an acrostic poem

Read the shape poem.

Egg
Yellow yolk
for my breakfast,
with dip-in soldiers.
I love eggy bread,
boiled, fried, scrambled,
or poached eggs... How do
you like your eggs?
"Made from chocolate,
of course!"

How to write a **shape poem**:
• Draw an outline of a familiar object.
• Write your poem inside the outline, following the shape.
• Don't worry about rhyme - it doesn't have to rhyme.
• Try to include alliteration, e.g. yellow yolk.

This circle shape could represent a ball, a bubble, the Sun or the Moon – you decide. Then write a shape poem of your own inside the circle.

acrostic: A poem or other piece of text in which some of the letters spell out a word when you read downwards.

This is an acrostic poem. The first letter in each line spells a name.

My brother
Always kicking a ball or
Running recklessly
CRASH! Into me!
OUCH! Look where you're going!

Here's another example:

>   **P** L A Y F U L
>   **C U** T E
>   Y E L **P**
>   **P** A W
> F U R R **Y**

How to write an
acrostic poem:
* Write about something or someone that you know well.
* Spell out the subject of your poem vertically down the page.
* Alongside each letter continue with a descriptive phrase or word.

A

Write an acrostic poem of your own in the space below.

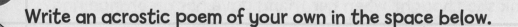

Settings

Learning objective: to write a description of a known setting

A setting is the place where the events in a story happen.

A

The story below is set in a girl's bedroom. Read the story, then answer each question below.

Everything matched: walls, bed, cushions, carpet, dolls – everything was either purple or pink.

Her princess bed was fluffed up with pretty pink pillows and purple sequins sparkled all around.

Rose-scented perfume filled the air and a bubbling, purple lava lamp gave off a soft, warm, purplish glow.

But the day a friend gave her a strange-looking orange ring her cosy, pink world would change forever!

1. What sort of a person would have a bedroom like this?

2. Circle any alliterations that you spot in the second paragraph.

3. What do you think she thought when her friend gave her an orange ring?

4. Do you think the ring is going to be important in the story? Say why.

Say this tongue twister:
Princess was pretty in pink!

Find a description of a setting in a fiction book.

Writers often set their stories in places that they know well e.g. places they've visited, school or work. But sometimes writers use historical settings or imaginary places.

B

Think about a place that you know well. For example, it could be your bedroom, classroom or friend's room.

Write words that describe what you...
see:
hear:
feel:
smell:
taste:

Now use your notes to write a short description.

How to write a description of a place:
• Picture the place in your mind.
• Imagine the sounds, smells and feel of the place.
• Write down your ideas in a clear order.
• Use adjectives to describe it.

Characters

Learning objective: to write a character description

Read the character descriptions and answer the questions below.

1. Grandpa Bob, old and gnarled, like an ancient oak, sits rooted in his armchair, surrounded by his books. Age has not dulled his sense of humour or his mind, which is still as sharp and clear as ever.

2. Auntie Deera was round and plump with a soft, sunny face. When she laughed, which was often, her tummy laughed too. Her favourite saying was, "You'll never guess what happened to me today…"

3. Zak was a terrible two-year-old and a tearaway at ten. Every day at primary school, his cheeky grin got him into and out of mischief. "It wasn't me!" he'd say.

4. Charlie's blue eyes are outlined with thick, black mascara. A skull tattoo on her arm makes her look hard but I know she's not.

A

1. Which of the characters is more likely to read books: Auntie Deera or Grandpa Bob?

2. Which of the characters is most likely to enjoy food? Say why.

3. Rewrite the description of Auntie Deera using opposite adjectives to change her character.
   Auntie Deera was _____ and _____ with a _____, _____ face.

4. Which of the characters is the youngest? Say why.

5. How old do you think Charlie is?

Try writing a description of me! What adjectives would you use?

B

Write a description for each of these characters. Describe their personalities and behaviour, as well as what they look like.

<u>Miss Harshly, teacher</u>

<u>Bulky Bazza, weightlifter</u>

<u>A.T., alien being</u>

Write a character description of someone that you know well.
Disguise their true identity by changing their name, as many writers do!

How to write a character description:
• Choose names carefully that suggests a character, e.g. Mrs Jolly.
• Ask yourself questions, e.g. What's their personality? What do they like to do?
• Different characters should speak differently, e.g. they might have favourite sayings.
• Give your character an unusual feature, e.g. eyes of different colours.

Story Plans and Plots

Learning objective: to learn how to plan a story

Now it's time to write your own story. Try these story-planning tips:

1. Choose a book you have enjoyed and imitate it. Changing the setting, the characters and the events.

> For example: you could write a story based on The Three Billy Goats Gruff but change the troll to a bully and the Billy Goats Gruff to you and your friends!
>
> I was walking home from school with Gaz and Tim when we saw him, swinging on the gate.

2. Retell something that has happened to you but change the characters and the setting.

> For example: write a story based something you lost. Perhaps it belonged to someone else!
>
> Where could it have gone? I'm in big trouble now. Mum doesn't even know I had it!

3. Use more than one theme, e.g. good and evil, friendship, lost and found, a long journey, rags to riches.

> For example: write a story that explores two themes - friendship and rags to riches.
>
> Cindy carried her empty suitcase to the station. She pretended it was heavy so that the others wouldn't know she had nothing to put in it.

52

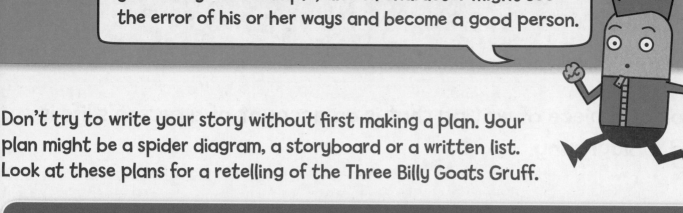

The characters should be changed by the events in your story. For example, an evil character might see the error of his or her ways and become a good person.

Don't try to write your story without first making a plan. Your plan might be a spider diagram, a storyboard or a written list. Look at these plans for a retelling of the Three Billy Goats Gruff.

The Troll and the Three Billy Goats (retold)

Storyboard

Billy goats teasing troll	Troll lonely	Small billy goat falls
Troll saves him	Making friends	Troll is happy

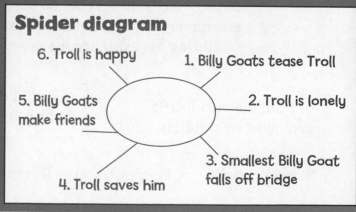

List

1. Billy Goats tease Troll.
2. Troll is lonely.
3. Smallest Billy Goat falls off the bridge.
4. Troll saves him.
5. Billy Goats make friends with Troll.
6. Now Troll is happy.

Spider diagram

6. Troll is happy
1. Billy Goats tease Troll
5. Billy Goats make friends
2. Troll is lonely
3. Smallest Billy Goat falls off bridge
4. Troll saves him

Now try planning and writing your own story on a separate piece of paper.

Biography

Learning objective: to understand how to write a biography

A book or a piece of writing that is an account of a person's life is called a biography.

A The paragraphs below are all from the biography of Roald Dahl. But they are all mixed up. Read them carefully and then write the order you think they go in.

Biography of Roald Dahl (1916–1990)

1. After school, he worked for the Shell Petroleum Company in Tanzania and in 1939, at the start of the Second World War, he joined the Royal Air Force.

2. He recovered and resumed duties in 1941 but then he started to suffer from headaches and blackouts.

3. Sadly, when he was just four, his seven-year-old sister died from appendicitis and a month later his father died from pneumonia.

4. He began writing in 1942 after being sent home from the army. His most popular children's books include *Charlie and the Chocolate Factory*, *James and the Giant Peach* and *The BFG*.

5. In 1940, Dahl was out on a mission when he was forced to make an emergency landing. Unluckily he hit a boulder and his plane crashed, fracturing his skull and his nose and temporarily blinding him.

6. Dahl married in 1953 and had five children.

7. Roald Dahl was born in Cardiff in 1916, the son of Norwegian parents.

I think that the paragraphs should go in the following order:

DEFINITION

timeline: A line representing a period of time on which dates and events are marked.

B

Write a biography of a friend or relative. Use this space to plan a timeline of their life writing key events above the line and dates below it.

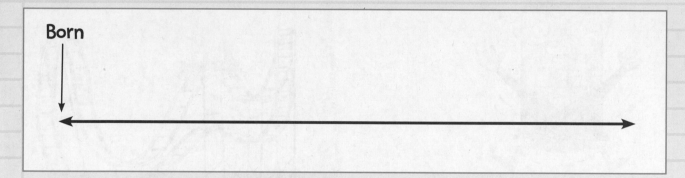

Born

Now write the biography in this space:

Read the snippets of text taken from an advertising leaflet for Awesome Towers.

AWESOME TOWERS!

- Have you got what it takes to ride the biggest rollercoaster?
- Special holiday season tickets
- Park and ride
- Gift shop
- New this year!

AWESOME TOWERS!

- A fabulous day out for all the family!
- There's something for everyone...
- Fantastic fun-packed activities for all ages.
- Ride awesome rollercoasters.
- Watch spectacular live shows.
- Enjoy an excellent choice of cafés and restaurants.
- You're guaranteed to have fun!

Next time you visit an attraction pick up a leaflet and notice how it is written.

A Now write a leaflet advertising a major attraction near you.

Amazing day out! Come rain or shine!

Holiday discount prices

Buy one ticket, get one free!

How to write persuasive text:
- Use adjectives, e.g. biggest, best, terrific, exciting, guaranteed, great.
- Use verbs, e.g. enjoy, see, find, discover, watch, ride, go, eat.
- Speak to the reader, e.g. use the pronoun 'you'.

Writing a review

Learning objective: to write a review of a book, song or film

Read the book review below. Notice how it is set out under different headings.

<u>Title:</u> Kensuke's Kingdom
<u>Author:</u> Michael Morpurgo

<u>Brief outline of the story</u>
The story is about a boy called Michael and his family who set off to sail around the world. One stormy night, Michael and his dog get washed overboard. They are rescued by Kensuke, an old man who lives on a desert island.

<u>Strengths</u>
I liked the way the author wrote about the friendship between Michael and Kensuke. It seemed very real, like a true story.

<u>Weaknesses</u>
I think it was sad at the end when Michael left the island. I usually prefer stories with happier endings. But if Michael had stayed, his parents would have been unhappy.

<u>Recommendation</u>
This is a wonderful book. Children over 8 years old would enjoy it, as I have.

<u>Score</u>
9/10

DEFINITION

review: An opinion or criticism of something.

Write a list of your top three books, songs and films.

A

Write a review of a book, a song or film that you have enjoyed.

<u>Title:</u>
<u>Author/artist:</u>
<u>Brief outline of the story</u>

<u>Strengths</u>

<u>Weaknesses</u>

<u>Recommendation</u>

<u>Score</u>
    /10

How to write a review:
- Give details about the book/song/film.
- Write about the things you liked.
- Write about the things you didn't like.
- Give a recommendation: say who would enjoy it.

Answers

Page 6 Spelling skills

A

spark, sparkle, sparkler
clear, cleared, clearly
bedroom, bedstead, bedtime
sign, signal, signature

Page 7

B

1. eight 2. hear 3. right 4. Would 5. Where 6. beach

Page 8 Important spellings

A

The month after April is May.
The shortest month is February.

Page 9

B

first, second, third, fourth, fifth, sixth, seventh, eighth, ninth, tenth

Page 10 Nouns and plurals

A

sausages, cakes, drinks, books, horses, trees
dishes, kisses, foxes, lunches, buses, wishes, crosses
ponies, babies, stories, daisies, cherries, berries

Page 11

B

buds, millions, flowers, sandcastles, leaves, trees, snowmen

C

1. There are mice in the house! 2. There were only two loaves. 3. We saw geese in the park.

Page 12 Prefixes and suffixes

A

untie, unlock, unlike, unlikely, unable, unfair, undo, unlucky, unhappy, unhurt
I'm very unhappy with you. It's so unfair! I'm just unlucky!

Page 13

B

Tom and Jez went to see a remake of Monsters of the Deep. Writing about it
in a movie review for their school magazine, they said, "The monsters were unrealistic and unimaginative really. There was lots of action but the plot was disjointed and impossible to follow."

C

1. thoughtful 2. useless 3. hopeful 4. careful

Page 14 Commas, questions, exclamations

A

1. We'll have two cornets with raspberry sauce, a vanilla ice cream, a carton of orange juice and a cup of tea, please.
2. I'd like to order the tomato soup, an egg and cress sandwich, a banana smoothie and a chocolate muffin, please.

B

1. The cat ran up the stairs, down the corridor, through the classroom and into Mrs Worgan's office!
2. Go right at the lights, turn right again at the T-junction, then first left.

Page 15

C

1. Suddenly, all the lights went out!
2. "Aaaaaaaargh!" he cried.
3. Gina called out, "Hey, Tom! "
4. "What are 'gators?" she asked.
5. How do we know there's no life on Mars?

D

1. Tara cried, "Wait for me!"
2. "Do you think he's an elf?" said Taylor.
3. "Okay," said Sharon. "What's wrong?"
4. "Wow!" said Zac. "You're a genius!"

Page 16 Apostrophes

A

can't, couldn't, shouldn't, we'll, they'll, where's, she's, they're

B

1. Ben's shoes 2. My friend's book 3. The dog's lead 4. Joe's car 5. The cat's whiskers

Page 17

C

1. The girl's fish 2. The teacher's book 3. The family's television 4. The clown's red nose 5. The babies' pram 6. The dolls' house 7. The children's drawings 8. The men's race

Page 18 Nouns, pronouns, connectives

A

The <u>flowers</u> were pretty.
<u>Zak</u> was asleep.
I live in <u>London</u>.
The <u>girls</u> laughed.
The <u>food</u> was delicious.
My <u>sister</u> has a <u>laptop</u>.

B

1. The flowers were pretty so I put <u>them</u> in a vase.
2. Zak was asleep so I didn't want to wake <u>him</u> up.
3. I like London because <u>it</u> has an interesting history.
4. The girls laughed because <u>they</u> thought it was funny.
5. Chris and I went swimming. <u>We</u> had a great time.

Page 19

C

Possible answers:

<u>First</u>, after register we had a spelling test. <u>Then</u> we wrote animal poems. <u>Before</u> lunch, we had a visitor. It was Mrs White. She'd brought her new baby to show us. <u>After</u> lunch, we had games outside on the field. <u>But</u> (or <u>However</u>) <u>suddenly</u> it started to rain and we had to run inside. <u>Next</u>, it was our science lesson. <u>Finally</u>, just before home time we had a story.

Page 20 Adjectives

A

Colours: blue, lemon, scarlet, violet, indigo. Sizes: huge, ginormous, miniscule, average, narrow. Moods: sullen, raucous, excitable, angry, bored.

B

Possible answers:

1. We had a great time.
2. The pizza was <u>average.</u>
3. The giant stomped his <u>huge</u> foot.
4. It was a <u>hilarious</u> movie.

Page 21

C

black > white
bold > weak (or shy)
hazy > clear
hairy > bald (or hairless)
unusual > common (or normal)
scorching > freezing
expensive > cheap
popular > unpopular
delicious > horrible (or disgusting)
polite > rude

D

Possible answers:

1. A <u>fierce, big</u> dog came bounding up to her.
2. It was a <u>new/modern</u> table.
3. It was an <u>easy</u> job.
4. He was in a <u>sad/bad</u> mood.
5. She went <u>white</u> when she saw him.

Page 22 Verbs and adverbs

A

1. found 2. chased 3. leaped 4. ate 5. skidded, crashed (two verbs).

B

Possible answers:

1. The girl <u>grabbed</u> the ice cream.
2. The red team <u>lost</u> the race!
3. The family <u>hated</u> camping.
4. The children <u>bought</u> a cake.
5. The boy <u>walked</u> across the road.

Page 23

C

1. The cat <u>purred</u> **softly**.
2. The giant <u>sneezed</u> **loudly**.
3. The man <u>drove</u> **quickly**.
4. The sun <u>beat</u> **fiercely**.
5. She <u>sang</u> **beautifully**.

D

Possible answers:

1. The teacher spoke <u>angrily</u>.
2. The boy <u>hurriedly</u> wrote his name.
3. The car <u>slowly</u> came to a halt.
4. The children played <u>happily</u>.
5. I sneezed <u>loudly</u>.

Page 24 Tenses

A

1. It will rain on Wednesday.
2. It was sunny on Saturday.

B

Past	Present	Future
It was hot	It is hot	<u>It will be hot.</u>
I was hot	<u>I am hot</u>	<u>I will be hot.</u>

Answers

He was hot.
We were hot.
They were hot.

He is hot
We are hot.
They are hot.

He will be hot.
We will be hot.
They will be hot.

Page 25

C

I am painting — I painted
I am jumping — I jumped
I am shopping — I shopped
I am skipping — I skipped

D

I got out of the car and stepped in a puddle. We heard the band playing. They had started already! I ran all the way to the hall.

Page 26 Fiction and non-fiction

A

Volcanoes – NF
Primary Science – NF
Bedtime Stories – F
Teddy Goes to Toytown – F
A History of the Vikings – NF
Treasure Island – F

Page 27

B

A. Wizardy Woo B. Secrets and Spies C. Disappearing Worlds

C

Fiction: Wizardy Woo, Secrets and Spies
Non-fiction: Disappearing Worlds

Page 29 Fiction comprehension

A

1. It is about the first day of the sales.
2. The customers are waiting outside.
3. She is nervous about the opening.
4. They are 'like sharks around a carcass'.
5. She is 'like an underwater swimmer moving against the current', and 'like a seashell carried on a wave'.
6. There will be mayhem as the customers fight for bargains.
7. Any suitable title.

Page 30 Fables

A

Possible answers:

A dog was hurrying home with a big bone that the butcher had given him. He growled at everyone who passed, worried that they might try to steal it from him. He planned to bury the bone in the garden and eat it later.

As he crossed a bridge over a stream, the dog happened to look down into the water. There he saw another dog with a much bigger bone. He didn't realize he was looking at his own reflection! He growled at the other dog and it growled back.

The greedy dog wanted that bone too, and he snapped at the dog in the water. But then his own big bone fell into the stream with a splash, and quickly sank out of sight. Then he realized how foolish he had been.

Page 31

B

1. He was hurrying to get home quickly before someone stole the bone from him.
2. The other dog growled back because it was just a reflection.
3. The dog learned that he had lost his bone because he was greedy.
4. b) It is foolish to be greedy.

Page 33 Alliteration

B

REUSE AND RECYCLE
DANCING DOGS IN SCHOOL DRAMA
TWINS ARE A TERRIBLE TWOSOME
LOOK AFTER YOUR LONG LOCKS

Page 34 Classic poetry

A

1. The extract tells us about the rats.
2. killed/cats/cradles; bit/babies.
3. vats, sprats, hats, chats, flats.
4. A ladle is a big spoon.
5. The apostrophe tells us that there is only one cook.
6. They all begin with an 's' sound. They also rhyme.
7. Hats worn on Sunday when going to church.
8. 'With shrieking and squeaking
In fifty different sharps and flats.'

Page 36 Nonsense poems and limericks
A
1. Bald, all.
2. Thinner rhymes with dinner. When we eat we usually grow fatter so growing thinner is a sign that the Vulture isn't well.
3. The poem teaches us not to eat between meals.
4. It is not a serious poem but a fun or nonsense poem. The Vulture doesn't have a bald head and thin neck for the reasons given in the poem.

Page 37
B
1. Quickenham and sickenham are both made-up words, invented to rhyme with Twickenham.
2. She wore the boots for a time before she took them off.

Page 39 Playscripts
A
"A new puppy!" Buster wailed. "After everything I've done for them."

"I knew you'd be upset," replied Sindy. "I said to our Mindy when I heard."

"I take them for lovely walks, I eat up all their leftovers – even that takeaway muck they always dish out on a Friday... and this is the thanks I get!" said Buster.

"You can choose your friends but you can't choose your owners," said Sindy, sympathetically.

"What can they want a puppy for anyway?" cried Buster.

"Well, puppies are cute," said Sindy.

"Cute! Aren't I cute enough for them?" replied Buster.

"Er ...," said Sindy.

"Well, I'm telling you now," said Buster. "It's not getting its paws on my toys. I've buried them all!"

Page 40 Formal letters
A
1. She needs to leave at 2.45 pm in order to get to the appointment on time.
2. Becky's appointment is on Tuesday.
3. Mrs Kenwood apologises because Becky will miss a lesson.
4. Becky will have to do her homework because Mrs Kenwood is going to collect it.

Page 41
B
1. The kitchen company's address is on the left.
2. Shoddy means careless and of poor quality.

3. Mrs Kenwood wants the company to put right these mistakes.
4. She is exasperated, disappointed and annoyed.

Page 42 Instructions
A
1. You need a plastic bag, rolling pin, glass.
2. No there isn't enough for two glasses because the ingredients state 'serves 1'.
3. No, because the apple slices are for decoration only.
4. These words are verbs.
5. Any appropriate name.

Page 45 Information text
A
1. Philip was angry because she was a Catholic and he was too.
2. 'It was the final straw' means that Philip could not take any more.
3. The English ships could then be attacked on three sides.
4. The plan was to sail burning ships into them.
5. The English ships were smaller, faster and had better cannons.
6. The Armada was shipwrecked off the coast of Ireland and Scotland.
7. About 65 Spanish ships survived.
8. They all survived.

Page 48 Settings
A
1. A girl, about 9 years old. Someone who loves girlie things.
2. Princess, pretty, pink, pillows and purple; sequins and sparkled.
3. She was disappointed the ring wasn't pink or purple.
4. The ring is important because we are told that it would change her world forever.

Page 50 Characters
A
1. Grandpa Bob is more likely to read books.
2. Auntie Deera is most likely to enjoy food because we are told she is plump.
3. (possible answer) Auntie Deera was tall and thin with a sharp, sullen face.
4. Zak is the youngest because the text implies that he is ten years old.
5. Charlie is probably a teenager.

Page 54 Biography
A 7, 3, 1, 5, 2, 4, 6

Index